THE 7 PRINCIPLES OF TRANSFORMATION

ACCOMPLISHING YOUR GOALS WITH THE RIGHT INSIGHT..........

EMMANUEL GOSHEN

Published by Edson Consultancy

© Copyright Edson Consultancy 2015

THE 7 PRINCIPLES OF TRANSFORMATION

All rights reserved.

The right of Emmanuel Goshen to be identified as the author of this work has been asserted in accordance with the Copyright, Designs and Patents Act 1988.

No part of this publication may be reproduced, stored in a retrieval system, or transmitted, in any form or by any means, electronic, mechanical, photocopying, recording or otherwise, nor translated into a machine language, without the written permission of the publisher.

Condition of sale This book is sold subject to the condition that it shall not, by way of trade or otherwise, be lent, re-sold, hired out or otherwise circulated in any form of binding or cover other than that in which it is published and without a similar condition including this condition being imposed on the subsequent purchaser.

ISBN 978-0-9930661-7-7

Printed and bound in the United Kingdom

I would like to dedicate the success of this book to the Almighty God, the foundation and pillar of wisdom.

APPRECIATION

Except the Lord build the house, they labour in vain that build it: except the Lord keep the city, the watchman waketh but in vain *Psalm 127:1*. I offer my profound gratitude to the almighty God for His unlimited inspiration. I would like to thank my family (Beatrice, Rachel and Edward) and friends for their huge sacrifice in allowing me to write and publish this book; my mother, Pastor Mrs. Victoria Majekodunmi for her inspirational words in bringing me up as well as Prophet Akinfenwa and his family, Prophet Moses Olurin and his family for their support and prayers. I would like to thank Prophet Larry Osoffo, Pastor Eric Duru and Pastor Eric Amankwah for their unforgettable support. Dr Martin Ehigianusoe will always be remembered in my prayers for the time and effort he invested in making this book a reality. o Evangelist, Olusegun Olarinde, Mr and Mrs Obafaiye, Mr and Mrs Akinola. Mr and Mrs Ajibade, Mrs Janet Sims, Mrs Sarah Francis, Mrs Alayo, Pastor Akin Soyoye, Mr Abayomi Domingo, Mr Vicent Eni, Ms Toyin Ajose, Mrs Philippa Gittens and her lovely family - they are worth to me more than any kind of treasures and have a special place in my little heart. I will always remember them in my prayers. I wouldn't pass by without appreciating Pastor Yinka Ogunlola and his family, Mr David Taylor, Mr Loveday Cole, Mr Mich Boreman, Ms Busayo Asade Mr and Mrs Kuku for their huge and lovely support. Also, many thanks to Ionut C. Petrila, my proofreader, you are all wonderful and worth more than what mere words could describe.

ABOUT THE BOOK

Just like in his previous books, Emmanuel Goshen has taken a lot of time and effort to put together all the necessary information about leadership and its transformation. This book, in particular, is the best example of what transformation and leadership have in common and how they are unbreakably connected. In the beginning of the book, the author describes and defines the process of transformation and sets a clear approach about its importance in the business environment. It fully explains what kinds of strategies are needed in order to be successful and reach the desired goals. As popularly said, information leads to transformation, but only when the right processes and principles are applied at the right time and in the right manner. Most leaders fail to deliver what is expected of them due to the lack of insight and the right knowledge to transform the current situations in the desired state. This book facilitates leaders to create the strategic and critical thinking that is required in developing the rightful initiative in meeting the stakeholder's expectations. Therefore, this is a great handbook for executives and managers. Certain qualities and characteristics are needed in order to become a leader, and such attributes are fully described here. It is entirely made clear what identifying and embracing strategic initiatives means and what it takes for leaders to do so that they can run a triumphant organisation. The author also gives comprehensive and easy ideas on how to make such organisations sustainable to any challenges that might appear through time. This book is recommended for anyone that wants to run a sustainable and successful business because it is really easy to follow, and the advices given here are applicable in reality.

TABLE OF CONTENTS

ABOUT THE BOOK v
PREFACE 1
WHAT IS TRANSFORMATION? 5
THE NEED FOR TRANSFORMATION 11
FACTS ON TRANSFORMATION 15
WHAT IS TRANSFORMATIONAL LEADERSHIP? 23
PRINCIPLES OF TRANSFORMATION 37
PRINCIPLE 1: DEVELOPING A STRATEGIC MIND-SET 43
PRINCIPLE 2: HAVING A STRATEGIC MISSION 53
PRINCIPLE 3: INFLUENCING WITHOUT AUTHORITY 67
PRINCIPLE 4: DISCOVERING ONESELF 71
PRINCIPLE 5: IDENTIFYING AND EMBRACING STRATEGIC INITIATIVES 77
PRINCIPLE 6: BUILDING AND PROTECTING ORGANIZATION BRAND 89
PRINCIPLE 7: EMBRACINGINSPIRATIONAL LEADERSHIP 97
WHY TRANSFORMATION EFFORTS FAIL 105
TAKE THIS HOME 109

PREFACE

Margaret Thatcher, the former British prime minister, once said during her time in the office: "Do not follow the crowd. Let the crowd follow you." This statement truly reflects the purpose of becoming a leader. It is crucial to transform the current situation in life, rather than leaving things as they are or making them worse. This quote actually reflects that these leaders have to realize that *"making the crowd follow you'* requires one to be more influential, rather than being influenced by the crowd. This comes from the fact that only the leaders are those who are responsible for the consequences. It requires leaders to be courageous in facing the challenges and being able to make effective decisions that are in the interest of all of the relevant stakeholders, because the desire for transformation is always aimed at changing the whole organization and not just a portion of it. This really reflects effective leadership. Long story short, the transformation is all about making the right decision at the right time and at the right place.

Successful transformational leadership is also about making an incredibly strong case as to why the change is necessary at a particular point in time within an organization.

It is the unique form of leadership that promotes a common and reasonable vision in a simple and understandable manner. Such a vision establishes a successful pattern for continuous improvement and helps market leaders stay at the top. It would be best for transformational leaders to always remain inspirational, trustworthy, and charismatic role models. Furthermore, it is important that they display all the necessary qualities, so that they can serve as a positive reflection to the next generation, like, for an example Abraham Lincoln, the former president of United States, did. He will never be forgotten worldwide for the changes he had made and the legacy he had left behind. Lincoln led the United States through the Civil War in the time of a great moral, constitutional and political crisis.

Still, he had preserved the Union, abolished slavery, strengthened the federal government, and modernized the economy. Therefore, transformational leaders have to understand both strengths and weaknesses of their team and align them with tasks and goals that would optimise performance. They need to engage their team in activities that enable them to improve themselves, so they can become leaders later on.

Taking a look at the history of the British Broadcasting Corporation, it was established in 1922, with a staff comprised of only four members. The organisation began with a radio service, transmitting the national and sporting events during the 1930's. Later, in the mid 30's, it began its first television service. However, the Corporation began to boost as a result of competition with the other television channels which lead to its expansion. This expansion began with the introduction of new channels, such as world service radio, and it was complemented by BBC world television service. BBC later began to invest in the internet service channels such as BBCiPlayer, BBC app, kids' channel, i.e.CBeebies and CBBC and satellite channels which made it easier to transmit both events and information to and from any part of the world. However, all the periodical changes did occur in the light of new technologies, as a result of the internet revolution. The changes also required the operational structure to execute various tasks. Another positive aspect of the whole process was that the organisation had to acquire more buildings and offices around the globe so that they could deliver an expected service for its stakeholders. In the end, the organisation was transformed from its previous state in the 1930's to its current state. To meet up with challenges and expectations, leaders have to be able to transform.

To succeed, transformational leaders need to ensure that they've gotten the right strategic vision, which is critical for the smooth planning and implementation of any transformation process. Another advice for the leaders is to ensure that their platform is well placed for the proper execution. The achievement of the desired business results reflects the responsiveness and effectiveness of the leaders. As it was mentioned in "The Seven Laws of Productivity": "stakeholders depend rather on the previous results, then on the current ones, which could give a bright reflection of their expectation for the future of their investments." As a matter of fact, leaders cannot be wedded to a past or current success but should always seek methods to improve themselves, which is and remains the biggest challenge in transformation. Senior or executive managers should always keep in mind that the customers would always need more than just an introduction, whether it is a new product, or rebranding existing products or services in a marketplace.

This book explains what transformation is and what it's not. It explains the facts and various aspects of transformation. The need for transformation and transformational leadership alongside with already tested and proven Seven Principles for transformation were examined as well. Realistic study of the role and impact of strategy, innovation, smart planning and leadership as a whole was also performed. In order to succeed, there are some recommendable tips to sustain transformation over a long period of time.

WHAT IS TRANSFORMATION?

As accustomed in everyday phenomenon, the increasing need for transformation has become an important aspect in life. However, the more we grow, the more our minds become equipped in our approaches towards humanity. Our level of maturity is expected to increase with the way we relate to each other, view and handle situations with little or no conflict. Changes in taste, fashion and processes can occur in one way or the other once we discover some new or unique substance. Transformation as a whole is a common expectation in human life, because if reflects our intelligence and capabilities in terms of how many contributions are being made towards creating a positive impact in reality. Transformation needs to be embraced, especially today when the business environment is constantly changing and the competition is increasing in the marketplace. The demand for innovative products has caused organisations to compete with their rivals and to struggle for a better and stable position in the marketplace. Due to the doubtless fact that organisational stakeholders and investors are always seeking for realistic ways to keep their investments and interests stable, the need for transformation seems to be more realistic which has caused leaders and senior managers to be more visionary, critical, and strategic. Leaders are also more innovative in their thinking and perspective in meeting the demand and taste of the customers, so they would feel like royalty. This very challenging and increasingly important role of research and development in helping organisations meet the changes in taste, fashion and demand of customers and platform for discovering new products and operational processes is constantly increasing. Transformation is not just about the change in organisation process. Nowadays, leaders are well-known for two things: 1. The problems they have created; and 2. The problems they have solved. However, both outcomes have a remarkable impact on the investment and the constantly improved relationships with other stakeholders such as employees, suppliers, customers and partners because it determines how strong an organisation could stand up to challenges in the long run. In terms of recognizing the need for transformation, leaders need to use effective and constructive communication, as well as change their terms to identify both current and potential challenges. Whatever is at stake, taste or quality of the product, branding or any other factor, it needs to be analysed to confirm to the need of both internal and external stakeholders, and later generate various ideas which are realistic and in line with solving the problem. In most cases, existing solutions can be implemented directly, while in some cases ideas need to be developed and made up, which requires further developments of relevant components to secure a proper transformation. This means relying on certain conditions, factors or components, which could determine the extent of the known solutions to transform an organisation. Having a brilliant idea and not implementing and developing it at the right time is similar to placing a delicious cake in the middle of a river, from which nobody benefits. During unpleasant times, calls for a change in leadership are made, yet successors usually fail simply because they were unable to change the internal causes that were major contributors to the unpleasant situation. Having participated in Consultancy Company and following certain project development, I realized the problem attached with transforming an organization is not the time allocated. The most common problems are the bureaucratic internal policies, processes and systems. This makes the situation harder for leaders and agents to implement new ideas. However, most of the policies that stay as an obstacle were designed as a result of a certain legislation that was made at a particular time and for a specific purpose. The fact remains, transformational leaders never give up as a result of iron bars disallowing the implementation of new ideas. They always seek alternatives. To some, an extended transformation is a changing process, yet, in some cases, it is seen simply a period with the purpose of creating a positive impact, which is in the interest of all, depending on the opportunity available at a particular moment. Transformation can be measured by the impact it makes within a certain organisation. That increases the chances of growth in terms of productivity, development in terms of the required skills and knowledge for continuous improvement and making transformational processes a reality. I personally see transformation in two different ways: as *power* and *light.* I see it as Power in the sense that it creates the avenue for empowerment and the insight that enables an individual to see himself as a gift to others. That also enables the leader to discover and develop the true gift in them; it implements positive thoughts in one's approach which broadens one's knowledge and possibilities. As a matter of fact, principle is not a matter of pretending to be something the one is not, or milking some famous people. The power of transformation is embracing the reality of discovering ones actual positive characteristics in handling situations and facing down challenges. A transformation would not happen personally, nor within an organization without leaders that are empowering themselves and others within, because it makes them fearless regardless of what comes their way. However, the actual principle of transformation can only be made real through empowerment by realizing the potential ways of getting things done, mostly during the tough times. Transformation as power enhances the courage for both leaders and their teams to believe in themselves, regardless of typical challenges and the external waves of competitors. The transformation could also be seen as a Light, due to its function in illuminating the ignorance that could cause shortfalls and disappointments in terms of stakeholder's expectations and service delivery. It becomes easier to execute strategies when the right and relevant information are gathered, and when we focus on a realistic direction as we follow an ideal transformational process. The light in any transformational process brings the clarity and creativity that strengthen the mind's capacity of seeing oneself and the organization as one. Having described transformation in terms of power and light as a matter of fact, I would like to clear the air regarding transformation in terms of principles. The value of a particular principle lies in its ability to command respect, be applied in tough times, andits power to stand the tests of both humanity and time. I see the principle of transformation as an avenue for leaders to manage and improve their performance, morale, motivation, and dedication towards exceptional outcomes or results. Many authors do classify transformation and change as the same due to their similarities in turning the situation around positively by implementing limited initiatives. However, *change is situational* because it might come across an organisation, depending on the needs of the specific units or departments. Change might occur as a result of introducing new technology devices in making operational processes act faster. That means the system might require a smaller workforce for the production unit, but, at the same time new workers for the marketing and sales unit. This is because new technology might improve production using a smaller workforce to support the operational process. Therefore, there would be a lot of products for sale that would force an organisation to recruit more marketing and sales staff. In some cases, the situation might require the training of existing production staff to become familiar with the new technology or employ more people due to expansion of the production unit. Transformation on the other hand, unlike change management, does not focus on a fraction of an organisation, but rather on the overall goal to reinvent the organization and discover a new or revised business model based on a vision for the future. This means it might be adapting a new model or approach. However, transformation requires a well detailed strategic plan because it entails much higher risk and the future might be unpredictable due to unforeseen changes in external factors.

THE NEED FOR TRANSFORMATION

However, transformational leadership is the type of leadership aimed at creating positive impact, due to its ability to foster increased capacity and development levels within various aspects of an organisation. It is up to leaders to seek various improvement parameters in the areas of team-building, motivation and collaboration at different levels of an organization to fully accomplish the transformation. Transformation is more concerned with maintaining and upgrading operational processes effectively. It is not all about "keeping the ship floating" or changing its position, but making the situation of the ship more meaningful which enhances the ship to create a positive and an outstanding impact for its stakeholders. Transformation never occurs in the interest of one, but in the interest of all. That is why parameters such as goal setting and incentives recommendation are most likely to ensure higher performance from all stakeholders. All of that is possible in line with a common interest and that provides the opportunity for personal and professional growth within an organisation. Transformation needs to stand the test of time, cost, efficiency and durability so that the created impact is able to be outlined and clarified. In a nutshell, it is not all about just making an impact. It is about creating a positive, meaningful and an outstanding impact to all organisational stakeholders, as well. Some of the organisational leaders believe in "robbing Peter to pay Paul", and from experience, these leaders make little impact on a short run and later they fail due to the exposure of their incompetence and because of their previous cover up's in which they have exposed a negative picture of themselves.

It's up to leaders to understand the purposes of transformation that would enable the establishment of the critical parameters in achieving it within the expected time frame. It also entails the ability for leaders and managers to effectively manage the present state by exploiting the best practice in the past. This is based on setting and maintaining the updated and appropriate ethical and operational standards, like the need to respect relevant legislations. Understanding the mission of transformation requires the appropriate skills and knowledge to execute process as expected, mostly in the aspect of training and developing future talents.

Investing wisely and reasonably in the future is a perfect reflection of leaders that understand the process of transformation. It is all about empowering an organization by allowing leaders, managers and team member's to remain confident in a search for improvement. For example, taking action and assuming responsibility through delegation within an organisation as a whole.

However, wise investment in transformational activities makes it easier to face challenges fearlessly, which is another form of motivation. An origination investment would enable the exploration of new ideas and innovation practices. Also, it can help develop new capabilities fitted to specific contexts within an organisation, rather than just importing systems and routines from other contexts.

FACTS ON TRANSFORMATION

Transformation creates new paths in terms of organizational direction of developing new capabilities for both internal and external intentions. Effective transformational processes do make it possible for organizations to achieve "disruptive innovation". This is confirmed in a situation when the market is moving forward because of the well disposed of a newly-discovered product or the introduction of a new kind of service. Eventually, this leads to displacing already-established competitors with a sustainable advantage. It is required of any leader or change agent to understand the importance and impact of the three major components of transformation to attain successful implementation. Otherwise, once the pillars are down the roof follows. Transformation is not about miracles or magic. It is just a periodical and functional process that requires a lot of patience to materialize. Leaders need to be extraordinary cautioned while planning and implementing transformational process by avoiding unnecessary delay. The major components are: communication, stakeholder management and performance management.

COMMUNICATION

For change to occur in reality there must be an agreement within parties involved or affected, and the only tool available to share views and interests among the parties is communication. It facilitates mutual understanding and reduces the tendency of conflict among stakeholders. However, most strategies somewhere down the line fail as result of failure in communication. Later, this interrupts operational processes and might lead to a breakdown that leads to valuable resources being wasted. It is of prime importance for leaders to understand that communication is a two-way process that requires the exchange of thoughts and opinions. That also includes transmitting information by speech, writing, or symbols in order to achieve a mutually-accepted goal or outcome. This is vital for the transformation to be successful. Communication enables leaders and everyone in the process to translate and interpret information broadly and accurately in order to achieve operational success. Without this, communication visions can never be achieved.

The major purpose of effective communication is to help both leaders and organisations achieve sustainability and maximum efficiency in their relationship with both internal and external stakeholders. It requires effective communication to deal with the obstacles or opposition against implementing the necessary changes for transformation to be active. This really enables parties to understand the cause of the problem that the organization will be faced with and find the best way to apply new approaches. Communication remains a vital aspect to stay updated and persistent. This is a major indicator of an organisation leadership and management stands" for and against".

Having clarity about the goals and objectives that is intended to be accomplished is another impact of effective communication. This is accomplished by establishing a governance structure with clear roles and responsibilities. It is important to conduct a necessary audit to determine the existing internal and external resources and channels so that the opportunities for new positioning in the industry can be identified. Communication helps in creating an accurate feedback mechanism ensuring that the strategy is achieving its goals at periodical intervals. It is also needed in order to identify the need for continuous improvement, mostly when the changing direction is considered as a whole.

STAKEHOLDERS MANAGEMENT

Stakeholder management is the process of studying and identifying stakeholder groups, their interests, and the amount of stakes they possess. This also concerns determining if they represent inhibiting or supporting factors toward the transformation. It is the foundation of an effective organisational goal setting, all in line with the roles and responsibility that are required. It is also referred to as the formal management of the human dimensions of changing because it depends on how their needs are negotiated and satisfied. The objective of stakeholder planning and management determines who the stakeholders are and how they should be dealt with. Without them, leadership cannot work because they are a pillar of the organization. Leaders need to ensure that all stakeholders are appropriately represented and involved in the activities that lead to a strategic decision making. Stakeholder management is an initiative that requires a deep level of trust because it is about building relationships with everyone who can be affected by making the strategic decisions, mostly when an alternative route to success is in mind, as that might cause a reduction of inputs or change the quality of products or services. The role of the stakeholder management will always remain vital because it provides access to a wide range of views, expertise, values and beliefs, which can be integrated into the transformation service.

Stakeholders are a critical asset that may have a significant impact on transformation initiatives due to their power to protect their interest regarding their expectation and to reject an initiative if it seems that it is not in their interest. Stakeholder analysis is an effective method for enabling different stakeholder groups to understand each other's perspective and concerns. Establishing a trust and credibility throughout the process from planning and gathering information to analyse in presenting data is critical because this ensures that the findings are valued and acted on without any form of bias.

PERFORMANCEEXCELLENCE

Leaders need to place excellence at the peak of every effort they intend to make. The credibility of a leader is valued by the result of the accuracy in the implementation process. The foundation of excellence is always laid through a vision, values alignment; best practices and the relentless pursuit of improvement are the leading roles in the foundation of excellence. Leaders, who stick to the traditional ways of getting things done, usually find it difficult to sustain their organizations because their chances of attaining excellence are always slim. Without excellence, an organization would not just lose its financial resources, but the knowledge and employees as well and it will end up with little or no competitive edge. In a nutshell, performance excellence is often described as an outstanding practice in managing the organisation and achieving results, all of which is based on a set of fundamental concepts of values.

Performance excellence is the key to create an engaged and aligned relationship, which is the hallmark of all successful businesses. Tim Jones, a marketing consultant, points it out on a regular basis that excellences are the major key in acquiring more clients, furthering the development of the business, and forging new alliances. One's story is worth hearing because it shows the outer world of one's previous achievements and one's capability, which shows what one can do in terms of benefits. However, it deals with the alignment of visions and values, feasibility resolution for new endeavours and strategic market evaluation for strategic positioning within the marketplace. Performance excellence aims at focusing on what is the best for the future in terms of sustainability. This requires the understanding of the short and long-term factors that might affect an organization and marketplace. The desire for excellence facilitates sustainability of growth and effective leadership that are all about having a strong orientation for the future and the willingness to make long-term commitments to the satisfaction of all of the stakeholders. The necessity to understand performance excellence enables leaders to have a deep insight and focus, and it also aids in the development process of future leaders. That needs to include the accomplishment of effective succession plans. The desire for excellence also creates new opportunities for innovation, which increases the chances of improving existing products, services, programs, processes, operations, and business model. Performance excellence can also create new forms in adding value for the organization's stakeholders.

WHAT IS TRANSFORMATIONAL LEADERSHIP?

Transformational leadership emphasizes the behaviour that inspires nurturing others. It is a model of Leadership that meets both the challenges of a rapidly-changing environment and also the need to emotionally engage everyone within the organisation. It enhances a positive impact on the reputation of the organisation to both existing and potential stakeholders and clients.

Transformation is the only thing that enables leadership to attain different levels at expected interval, due to the renewal of the process all across an organisation in order to achieve the desired goal. No style of leadership could be classified as transformational without possessing the elements of integrity and fairness in acting beyond expectations. The major aim of transformational leadership is to improve performance, morale, motivation, and dedication of organisational stakeholders to promote the common interest and a realistic vision. In most cases, transformational leadership does create a strong case for positive impact inside the organisation.

Transformational leaders are often known to be inspirational, trustworthy, and charismatic, and this makes others, mostly the younger generation, see them as role models. They are known to lend a helping hand, especially in situations where they understand the strengths and weaknesses of their team members. They consider this a huge sense of responsibility because they want to ensure that nobody is left behind in terms of performance delivery. In most cases, it is advisable for group team members to give support in order to allow such optimized performance.

However, the function of transformation within the organisation goes beyond recommending and effecting a change in the existing operational process. Transformation also creates a strong and better platform for other values and opportunities. In terms of expectation, it yields more results for the purpose of survival. The desire for transformation is the major avenue for a leader. He or she needs to create an inspiring and a meaningful vision for the future regarding the team and organisation they lead. However, they have to keep in mind that high expectations require high spirits within the organisation.

Leaders need to have a prefect insight of what transformation is, because that gives them the required confidence to draw up a realistic operational and strategic process. These actions are generating more clients and increasing revenue. Leaders need to test transformational processes on a small scale before investing as this extends the scope for various advantages. Once we comprehend what are the demands in a certain situation, it becomes easier to identify new opportunities regarding the market and new clients. Transformation is the type of organizational process that enables leaders to get more out of their existing client, because it strengthens its relationships by creating a fantastic service delivery. This increases clients' trust in sustaining existing projects as agreed without any form of fear or doubt. Transformation is the backbone in achieving excellence and it serves as a form of presentations to court potential clients. For organizations to remain at the top, there is a need for leaders to continuously seek the parameters for improvement, both internally and externally. The process of transformation as a whole enables leaders to set realistic and effective personal goals, which makes them remain positive in attaining milestones, mostly during the challenging periods. Transformation requires effective strategies to make goals more flexible to achieve, mostly when it is adapting to changing circumstances. It is impossible for all the people that make an organisation to have or expand their comfort zone without benefitting from an effective transformational process. For transformation to occur, it is necessary for one to make up his or her mind, attack their fear to be able to leave the comfort zone and take bold steps while heading towards a desired growth zone. Most people prefer their comfort zone due to the fear of loss. Getting out of the comfort zones also means not listening and taking wrong advice from friends, family and hearing fearsome news and information from media channels and various headlines. Most people say half bread is better than none, due its consistency, but this also means settling for less while forgetting the upcoming disappointment. However, transformation requires both organisations and leaders to think and stretch beyond and outside the box, without limiting one's ability to face the current and upcoming challenges. As a matter of fact, leaders need to engage in continuous learning and uprising for the purpose of informing and pushing themselves towards relevant changes. That remains a parameter which enables them to reach new heights and also to realize what their full potential is. Stretching out of comforts zone would always put leaders or anyone in the situations where they can grow and build effective skills and knowledge in order to achieve their goals. They gain enough experience to stand on their own and to be able to coach others later on. As previously mentioned, transformation creates the path in gaining the required confidence and having the perfect mind set towards achieving one's goals and loosing those beliefs that holds them back from taking steps. Fear destroys a vision faster than explosive.

Another important aspect of transformation is its ability to ensure that leaders inspire them and their team to move forward in certain situations, which is in the interest of all stakeholders. This is about generating new and relevant ideas in order to increase the level of success within the organisation. Leaders need to comprehend how to manage unexpected issues and challenges as they could make them omit some opportunities that will wind up as a bonus for their competitors.

Specific situations need to be taken into serious valuation before organisational processes are transformed. This includes: **1.**Setting clear and realistic expectations;**2.** Encouraging others to make a commitment in sharing the vision of their leader and **3.**Contributing their part in getting things done. However, leaders need to ensure that the accurate operational support is in place so that the members do not feel abandoned by rousing their emotions. Developing a culture of collaboration, where change is welcomed as an opportunity is better than a form of command and control with a threat as the main motivation .Another aspect leaders need to work on is to reflect that the transformational process is beyond their self-interest. It is more about the constantly investing in the development of themselves and others, which is a platform for recognizing effective leadership. This needs to be demonstrated and maintained at all times within an organisation.

Transformational leaders are well known for their ability to cherish the commitment within their team in attaining goals and heights. In a nutshell, transformational leadership is about achieving the goals through new approaches. It is also about creating value. Bear in mind, the goals need to be a part of a specific standard which enhances individualized consideration. It is important to identify the needs of the various members within the team they lead. They also need to encourage creativity by providing intellectual stimulation, which is a platform for fostering innovation and transformation. This is executed by challenging assumptions regarding the execution of processes that require supporting, providing and unitizing resources effectively, and also in removing the barriers in making changes come to life.

In general, various authors and writers in the field of Transformational Leadership had always come with the ***"Four I's"*** of transformational leadership. Peter Northouse defines leadership as a process whereby one individual influences a group of individuals to achieve a common goal. For effective leadership to occur, the role of influence cannot be underestimated due to its positive approach in reaching the goals of the organization. This is visible through its ability to persuade and motivate others to reach an understanding, mostly during the challenging moments. Furthermore, this approach can help managers become exceptional leaders due their ability to relate with others by using the four approaches. This is aimed at getting people to embrace change, to improve themselves and to be led with some new techniques.

The four characteristics of transformational leadership are popularly known as the four pillars of transformational leadership. This includes:

1. IDEALIZED INFLUENCE

This is an approach that makes others see leaders as being charismatic in their style. It is about building confidence in others and making their behaviour unique and principled, mostly in the terms of encouraging their vision for growth and stability. Leaders are seen as role models, because their behaviour inspires others to follow due to the high level of trust and respect they earn. That is what enables them to make better decisions via support given by their associates. However, there is a huge need for consistency in promoting the vision and values of an organisation by creating a way for team members share their thoughts in the form of suggestion. It becomes easier to create confidence in stakeholders if a serious commitment is shown towards achieving the goals of the organisation. For a leader to be of great influence, he or she would have to see the importance of facing challenges, while hanging onto others, rather than avoiding them. The major need for influence in transformational leadership is due to its ability of representing an organization's goals, culture and mission, which gives it a better reputation. Idealized influences about articulating a vision and explaining how to attain that vision in an appealing manner. Some authors refer to it as " leading by example", as it enables leaders to act confidently and optimistically in dealing with the challenges by sharing the risks with other team members and stakeholders. It is also about emphasizing values and reinforcing them by symbolic actions, as well as displaying a high level of ethical and moral conduct. Leaders who apply idealized influence within their team gain the trust, commitment and confidence of their team members.

2. INTELLECTUAL STIMULATION

This comprises of various manners of leadership that encourages individuals to come up with different ideas of getting things done along with the current ones. However, encouraging team members' creativity with each individual having an independent and different insight may cause problems. Producing consistent innovations by challenging the status quo is generating alternative solutions for complex problems. Intellectual stimulation facilitates in taking risks so that the leaders and their team can achieve desired goals.

By rocking the boat and asking questions, transformational leaders are always challenging the status quo and aren't afraid of failure. They foster an environment where all team members feel valued and where it is safe to have conversations, be creative and express ideas. They challenge the existing cultural norms and inspire passion for work in their team. The bottom line remains: Intellectual stimulation encourages innovation and creativity.

Transformational leadership encourages changes through intellectual stimulation, aimed at self-reflective change of values and beliefs. Transformational leaders raise the awareness of problems within their team members and they are also developing their capabilities to solve such problems by fostering a climate that favours critical examination of commonly held notions, beliefs, and the status quo. This is also achieved by creating an environment that is conducive to the creation and sharing of knowledge, as well as encouraging innovation and creativity ideas and heightening sensitivity to environmental change.

3. INDIVIDUALIZED CONSIDERATION

This is the platform for coaching individual members according to their specific needs. It goes along with a level of emotional intelligence that enables leaders to give support to them so that the improvement and productivity is enhanced. Commonly said, we are equally born, but differently talented, therefore individuals are motivated and excited by different things. As a matter of fact, leaders need to accommodate the difference of various team members in order to get their best performance. Leaders need to act as mentors or trainers to encourage and empower others by first listening and later attending to their concerns by showing genuine compassion, discussing and empathizing with the individual's situation. They should also make an interpersonal connection with their team members to facilitate an on-going professional development and personal growth, all for the upgrading of the organisation.

It's about listening to each team member's needs and concerns, and expressing words of gratitude and praise, as a way of motivation for the efforts that are made in attaining current levels. It is important to show that more effort is needed for the purpose of improvement. Ensuring fair workload distribution is also another attribute of intellectual stimulation.

4. INSPIRATIONAL MOTIVATION

This facilitates leaders in motivating others by remaining committed to the corporate organization's vision as a whole and understanding one's goals while considering the best strategy in accomplishing the desired level. Leaders need to reflect optimism and passion for their visions so the stakeholders acknowledge its importance in the big picture.

It is about getting in the minds of the people so that they can understand what tasks leaders are aiming to execute. Leaders with an inspiring visions challenge followers to leave their comfort zones, advocate optimism about future goals, and provide meaning for the tasks at hand. It is all about providing the energy that pushes a group forward in creating a positive impact within an organisation. The motivational aspect of transformational leadership facilitates in advocating the organization's vision by making it understandable, precise, powerful, engaging and worthwhile. Motivation could be seen as a train taking others to the future because it enables stakeholders to increase their willingness towards investing more effort in achieving the overall goal of the organisation. This act enables them to remain encouraged and optimistic about the future because it reflects the stakeholder's talents and worth. Inspirational motivation is a platform that inspires stakeholders to improve their performance for improved and expected outcomes. It explains the need to embrace change at a particular period and how an organization could benefit from transformational processes as a whole. It fosters a strong sense of purpose among stakeholders in the aspect of power, respect and influence and it enables them to achieve their potential.

The transformational leader inspires followers to create new ideas or goals through inspirational motivation. This is managed through the articulation of a clear and appealing view of the future and developing a shared vision in both economic and ideological terms so that the team members can get a picture of what is expected of them. It also facilitates in encouraging team members to integrate and become part of the overall organisational culture and environment.

The introduction and embracing of transformational leadership would create a path for innovations in developing and sharing an inspiring vision for the organization in the future. Leaders should behave in such manners that bring out the best out of individuals and team within an organisation. Showing a genuine concern and respect for others, continuous investment in the development and a culture of collaboration are rewards for transformational leadership.

The reputation of the organization is the results of consolidated experiences of many people over a period of time. It tells a lot of the organization's previous activities, their culture and their potential future. Transformational processes will affect the reputation of an organisation either positively or otherwise, because both existing and potential stakeholders depend much on it. An organisation's reputation also depends on the quality of its products, service standards, and merit of its staff and its place on the league table.

The reputation of the organisation determines how much investment a potential investor could make, because previous activities could be used in forecasting possible profits. Reputations often increases or falls the stake of an organisation based on the leaders' personal behaviour and conduct in public sight, skills and experience in making decision and attainting a specific direction. However, it often changes over time because of the unforeseen situations, news headlines, public assumptions and other external factors. Reputation is vital in promoting an organisation as a whole and it helps to survive the competition in the marketplace. Therefore, the reputation should be built on the behaviour of the organization as a whole and it should be based on the relationship with its existing customers. It should not be built with just branding or advertising as that might be deceitful sometimes. Both brand and reputation needs to be highly protected because it's the responsibility without justification.

PRINCIPLES OF TRANSFORMATION

Regardless of what the facts may be, the role of co-ordination cannot be underestimated in transforming an organisation and unless there is a team of individuals that have a mutual understanding, transformation would always remain difficult to achieve regardless of the resources invested in an organisation. Co-ordination makes it possible to understand the mission of the transformation and also its processes.

Coordination provides the path to exercise, analyse and discuss the strategic components in making the transformation materialized. Leaders need to attach every initiative to a clear purpose or goal. Transformation does not take place in a vacuum, it occurs in a specific place, at a specific time and for particular purposes. It requires coordination to align people, process and technology with the transformation initiatives to link its mission and vision. However, when they yearn for transformation is not being supported by stakeholders; it brings frustration and paralyzes the plan's execution because there is a lack of coordination in the system. Note, transformation never occurs in a comfort zone, because leaders need to strive to others to get things done as expected and make their capability and credibility justified and worthwhile. This reflects the major reason why leaders need not assume when facing challenging issues because a single mistake could cost them their career and reputation.

A political party won the fight over a local council after convincing the residents to transform its current state. After two years (out of a four-year mandate), only half of what has been promised was fulfilled. The political parties made a lot of high promises before the election, but the moment they took over the office, they were forced to face reality in terms of a real implementation and execution. The previous party had signed a long term contracts and some of them had to be re-negotiated. A lot of time was wasted before they reached an agreement. Others were terminated and that brought up a big number of court cases, which had cost the council a huge amount of money and resources. However, the reason for these actions was the future implications that would hinder the transformation to become real. The political party needed to ask from the centre government and other relevant agencies for changes in policies and other forms of concessions, in order to deliver their promises, which also took a lot of time. There was a huge need to review various policies, which were believed to have been a cause of major setbacks on a strategic basis. The bottom line is, things are easier to be said than done and the transformation is a process that is never easy to plan or discuss in the terms of execution.

I would like to suggest four major conditions that leaders need to understand and consider as best practices to transform their organisation to a desired state. The conditions stated below are to be applied alongside with the seven principles which would be discussed later in this book.

1. Leaders need to understand that operational processes must be capable of supporting and meeting stakeholder's needs. Every process should be able to play a vital role in increasing the value and reputation of the organisation, in light of competition. If an organisation aims at selling expensive goods for a smaller price and make it available for the middle class, such organisations need to consider and understand what kind of leadership strategy to entail, mostly in planning and operational wisdom. Embracing this leadership strategy could help organizations in creating a low-cost operation within their niche to gain a better advantage over competitors. This means reducing operation's costs below the costs of others within the same industry;

2. Leaders need to surround themselves with those who understand the mission of the organisation and consider the success of such as a major priority. Those people need to be able to support and execute the business and operational processes in achieving the organisational mission. Leaders would have to provide a better form of motivation through various mechanisms to enable them give their best. Transformational leaders are well known for influencing others towards efficacy based on their qualities, such as honesty, integrity and intelligence.

3. Transformational activities need to be executed in order to minimize the risk that can accrue on investment. Transformation needs to be simple, direct and understandable in terms of vision, which reflects the main reason for it. The planning process needs to identify its effects on the organisation as a whole. This refers to its benefits to various stakeholders, the possibility of eliminating or reducing barriers in making it a reality and recommending the possible remedies or alternatives. The ability of a transformational process to help the organisation minimize the risk and uncertainty creates a better chance for organisation to secure a strong path in the industry.

4. Measuring process and product quality. The measurement of the process and product quality permits an organisation to determine its range of possible changes, which can be used to evaluate the success of the effort in making changes. It also permits an organisation to compare the rate of actual change. Those are the seven practical principles of transformation.

However, leaders should never underestimate the role of team coaching, mostly in motivating and managing teams and other stakeholders in a period of change and uncertainty. Coaching enables leaders to effectively engage with their key stakeholders and jointly transform their organisation. This way they enable them to achieve their common purpose and performance objectives within a specific time frame. The bottom line remains, coordination enhances collective leadership and facilities transformation. Before explaining the principles one after another, I would like to share my experiences as a business coach that I have gathered over the years. I have to point out, that for every position, there is always an opposition, which is the major cause why organisational Leaders need to be strategic in their approaches and thinking. This requires them to remain defensive when they are on the leading side and to become offensive when they desire to edge out current market leaders. Strategic thinking facilities transformation because it enables leaders to see the organisation and the current challenges with a trained eye and a matured mind.

Stakeholders need to understand that the higher the intended building, the deeper and stronger the foundation needs to be. Likewise, the greater the impact of the intended transformation exercise, the tougher the challenges leaders face in which there is no point in seeing them as problems or obstacles but as positive steps towards achieving great expectations and writing their name in gold. Taking insight from the parable of the house on the rock in the bible, I strongly believe takes a perfect foundation begin laid before it would stand the rain, flood and wind and still retain its actual position, unlike the other house that was built on the sand. However, the seven principles of transformation are well explained and could be applied by anyone, mostly aspiring leaders. However, it essential for anyone applying those principles to believe in themselves and not give or stick to limitations and excuses but consider every challenge they face as a partway towards success.

PRINCIPLE 1

DEVELOPING A STRATEGIC MIND-SET

'The biggest risk is not taking any risk... In a world that is changing real quickly, the only strategy that is guaranteed to fail is not taking risks."(Mark Zuckerberg)

Having a strategic mind set is very vital in a leader's journey, because it is noted from various aspects that either success or failure is always a product or outcome of one's mind set. Taking insight from the Bible: *"As a man thinks in his heart, so is he".* It is not about the way someone else thinks or assumes about him or wants him to be. Having a better strategic mind-set impedes discouragement and never gives room for limitation. The marketplace is never a funfair centre, where leaders can afford to make decisions that are in the interest of their rivals. Leaders need the right and a prefect mind set regarding the strategic manner to make the best possible decisions. That stands in the interest of both their organisation and stakeholders. Having the right strategic mind set is the major parameter which facilitates the success behind any transformational process a leader wishes to inject into an organisation. I have lead various groups in the execution of various projects and discovered that greater achievements are products of inspired minds of the team members as this facilitates the pooling of efforts towards a specific goal which reflects effectiveness. A strategic mind set goes along with having a positive and a possible attitude towards challenges. For example, I have followed the documentary of the American retired professional basketball player, Tyrone Curtis, popularly known as "Muggsy" Bogues. He is the shortest player in the history of the NBA (height of 5'3"). He played along with the giants of about 7 feet or more and his performance during the game inspires me so much because his moves are fearless and powerful and his passes are accurate and unbelievable. During one of his granted interviews he said how he doesn't see himself as a short man during any game, i.e. he doesn't believe in impossibilities and does not fear to perform in any circumstances. His attitude during the game is always bold and does not give room for failure. He believes in himself and capitalizes more on his strength and passes the ball when the chances in making further moves are slim. He finds every task during the game as a challenge and stands up to it with a strategic and focused mind-set, which is the foundation and cornerstone of any success. Another vital point of the documentary was when the narrator explained his ability of making a positive impact to the younger generations. This came as the result of him not being afraid to take risks while playing.

It requires leaders to have the right mind set and long-ranged approach in solving problems and making decisions. This involves an objective survey, strategic thinking and planning. This provides the means for leaders to think within multiple time frames and in different dimensions so they can have an insight to the various outcomes of different plans on the board. It also enables leaders to compare the possible outcome after they identify the major task, standard and quality that need to be accomplished over a specific period of time. Developing a strategic mind set facilitates the leaders to act and think systematically because it orchestrates several coordinated change actions simultaneously. It also widens the perspective of leaders from the immediate goal to one that is considered for the entire system, i.e. identifying the impact of their decisions on various segments of the organisation before implementation, which includes internal departments, personnel, suppliers and customers.

For any organisation to be marked as successful, strategy formulation and execution seriously relies on clear choices made by leaders. Note: choices are the end product of one's mind sets, i.e. one's intention in a vision forms ahead any particular event. The same choices that are made need to be based on the deep understanding of the strategic context with ring – fencing the organisations ambition by relevant stakeholders. Otherwise, the transformation processes would end up as a one man's game, where a leader stages and lifts the trophy all by himself.

I believe in developing the right strategic mind set so much because it enhances the required strategic thinking for leaders and managers perform at their best. Transformation is a deeply impressive journey, and it explores the innovated and relevant specific strategic processes. This includes analysing the business environment, i.e. identifying the customers' needs in terms of taste and fashion and relevant legislations, which determine various activities both within and outside an organisation. This process also includes setting strategic goals to determine how the business obligations are met in the terms of creating satisfaction and value for money and claiming a better advantage over competitors.

In a nutshell, leader's mind set facilitates in the awareness of learning the practical and core principles that are required in advancing their knowledge towards understanding the steps in aligning their organization's performance with planned strategic outcomes. However, for transformation to occur leaders need to be equipped with the necessary tools to formulate, communicate and execute strategies that drive changes and sustain competitive advantage for its organisation.

It's important for leaders to know the best way to maximize their contributions in the strategic interest of their organisation, in terms of being concerned is the strategy effectively developed, communicated and implemented, mostly through the challenging periods in time. This gives leaders a winning edge and also reflects them as role models for others. The contributions brought by leaders make others understand how to plan and execute complex strategies to achieve goals, i.e. developing a stronger marketing and customer focus which is critical for the success of the organisation.

Having the right strategic mind set is the major work frame in applying the most advanced strategic planning methods in order to execute new initiatives in meeting the challenges that the organisation is facing with. It enables the development of a transition map that tracks operational progress within an organisation. However, nothing else positions one towards having the required ability to transform organisational situations for the best, other than having a strategic mind set which gives an accurate insight of what, how, when and where things should be done. It's all about understanding how value is created within an organization and how leadership effectiveness is enhanced.

In general, having a positive mind set and approach helps leaders to evaluate their abilities by exhibiting their strengths over their weaknesses in terms of comparing their capabilities with expectations and alighting where necessary action needs to be taken at the aim of improvement.

A major benefit of having a strategic and positive mind set includes the ability to: anticipate, challenge, interpret, decide, align and learn the processes of transformation in full context. In terms of anticipating, leaders need to focus on the strategic successes, not just the current ones. Such success induces the creation of values for customers, making them look like a "king". It also creates and develops more opportunities for the survival of an organisation. The term anticipates also reflects the ability to foresee changes within the industry in terms of threats and opportunities, knowing what is the best way to run business within the industry. Challenge simply refers to the conventional wisdom derived from questioning situation rather than accepting assumptions. It enables leaders to seek alternative measures in solving problems rather than accepting the problem as an outcome. Interpreting is always the result of anticipating change and challenging conventional facts. It is about understanding that everything must be thoughtfully analysed to yield actionable results. However, leaders need to compare and contrast outcomes from different aspects before arriving at conclusions. Making decisions is the first step in acting swiftly in taking courageous stands while balancing the speed between an organisation's present and future. However, it has to be in the interest of all relevant stakeholders in terms of standard, quality, and agility. In terms of aligning or alignment, leaders need to welcome the diversity of different opinions, but they also must know how and when to align divergent agendas to work towards a common goal. Actively engaging stakeholders to encourage open dialogue and address misalignment helps in building trust and reaching consensus for transformational purposes. In leadership, as a whole, the ability to learn from others and oneself enables leaders to go a long way, both in life and business. It enables leaders to see success and failure as sources with critical reflection or insight. Learning encourages and embraces feedback, which enhances the elements of reality in meeting and facing down future challenges.

Strategic mind set enables leaders to think, assess, view, and create a better future for themselves and for others.

It's an extremely effective and valuable tool that remains inevitable for any leaders to possess. However, it facilitates in making relevant decisions because it comprises a set of critical skills such as the ability to be logical and creative. Developing a strategic mind set enables one to have a clear insight of both personal and organisational vision, and it promotes the ability of focusing on critical components that could determine the success of one's practice. A leader with a focused and determined mind set are often known to be confident in their approach by placing their fear and possible disappointments aside and taking actions which are tremendously valuable. Nothing else would enable a leader to increase his perceptive rather than the ability to discover and recognize both internal and external parameters. These parameters could be of great importance in terms of guiding and communicating in a better direction for the future of an organisation. This is vital in terms of realizing and utilizing opportunities for a better strategic positioning within any industry.

Over the years and decades, it is recorded that leaders with a sound strategic mind are known to be good and fast strategic thinkers. They have the ability to clearly define their objectives and develop a strategic action plan with each objective broken down into tasks. Each task has a list of needed resources and a specific timeline with their desired goal. It's similar to targeting at one bird among others, not just aim at any, but a specific one because there is a specific reason for it. In a nutshell, having a strategic mind enables leaders to project and picture desirable achievements before execution. However, having a strategic mind is not about having *"I can do it all alone"* attitude, which is unethical. It is more about getting the required support to help others grow, which is a major attribute of great leaders. It is also about learning from everyone's experiences in order to transform. Another major characteristic of strategic thinkers is their ability to design flexibility into their execution plans by creating some benchmarks in reviewing potential and existing operational processes and progress that is attained at regular interval. Having a strategic mind or being a field marshal in one's discipline doesn't on its own guarantee success. They still need to be great listeners in order to get the inner parameter that could later serve as a cornerstone for the building to get the desired shape. Having and developing a strategic mind is the first and major step towards greater accomplishments because it gives a picture of what one intends to do and how to get it done. It enables the ability for leaders to be patient and not to rush to conclusions and judgments. Great ideas and thoughts require time to develop into a great success. Bigger challenges, distractions, difficulties and inaccurate information would always appear on the road in reaching one's defined vision, yet either success of failure is always the product of a person's mind set.

PRINCIPLE 2

HAVING A STRATEGIC MISSION

"Everyone has his own specific vocation or mission in life; everyone must carry out a concrete assignment that demands fulfilment. Therein he cannot be replaced, nor can his life be repeated, thus, everyone's task is unique as his specific opportunity to implement it."
(Viktor Frankl, 1905. – 1997.)

Having a nice plan and lacking the ability to place it in motion and towards a particular direction, is the easiest path of failure in leadership. This refers to the scenario in the book "LEADERS SUPPLEMENT" and the mission of getting the two diamond rings from the mouth of the lion, with the risk that one ring could be swallowed by the lion. Analysing the further situation, anyone backing on such mission should understand the specific challenge he might be facing, because the situation is never funny. That person needs to know the motive of such mission and have the insight on why it's necessary to go on such mission and what is required to fulfil it. It is either special training/

coaching or some basic skills. A reasonable mission needs to carry specific and tangible expectations; otherwise, all efforts would be rendered baseless. In most cases, the fear of the unknown weakens a person to the point he or she becomes unable to execute his or her vision. Making a vision become reality requires embarking on a strategic mission, i.e. processes with a tangible purpose which represents the vision. The primary purpose of embarking on a strategic mission is primarily to achieve the strategic goals in the long or short term. The major purpose for having a strategic mission is simply productivity because without it, an organisation would find it impossible to turn around its present situation to achieve the best result for customers and other stakeholders, while increasing profit margins. However, short term goals can't be underestimated because they sustain an organisation in some unexpected situations where some sales depend on external factors, such as climate or environment. The term transformation would only be recognised within an organisation if its leaders are able to formulate and put in place. Such effective operating process could succeed in reducing the level and quantity of waste, reducing production time by getting the required machines along with proper maintenance team to keep the operation flowing. This also includes making products and services available to the customer at the right time, in the right place and with the right quality. The mentioned situations represent the necessary renovations, which are expected to occur at all levels and aspects of an organisation in order to enhance effectiveness. These are the major steps towards transformation.

In most cases, the strategic mission is a long term approach because it entails plans which an organisation needs to operate so its vision, objectives and goals are achieved. However, leaders need to focus on external environmental factors due to the potential effect on the strategy, culture, and leadership of an organisation. They can force change to occur in the mentioned parameters and facilitate internal changes in organizational structure, systems, management practices and adjustment in financial and other forms of budgets. Having a strategic mission requires both leaders and organisations, as a whole, to understand their mission statement in practical context, which reflects their purpose as an organization and their benefit in relating to the outside world. Also, bear in mind that mission statements serve as yardstick that reflects standard and mode of operation and also serves as an internal indicator are leaders in or off course. Understanding the need and purpose of strategic mission enables leaders to inspire and motivate stakeholders continuously, provided that the strategic plan remains aligned with the overall goals, which ensures organisational success.

Apart from strategic and operational objectives, another purpose for embarking on a strategic mission in terms of transformation is innovation. Nothing else would enable organisations to be and stay ahead of their competitors, then the continuous research and development to create a new product or effective methodology in offering a better service in meeting the customer's needs. The drive-through banking system is another way of staying ahead of competitors because it meets the needs of customers by allowing them to withdraw cash and pay cheques without getting out of their cars, at any time of day. A friend of mine who works till late and receives his wages by hand finds it easier to deposit cash on his way from work. He had to switch his bank due to this value and benefit which is a competitive edge over his previous bank. However, a strategic mission without an agenda of creating value for clients and customer might suffer losses or setback in the long run in the marketplace. Innovation might occur in an organizations product or operational processes, but yet it requires a high level of initiatives.

It's impossible for any leader to embark on a strategic mission and produce a worthy outcome, without having the required initiative of what might occur and needs to be done. In reality, such leader might come across situations that might deny or delay from fulfilling such mission. However, no stakeholder is ready to pay for or take the excesses regarding the expected returns for their contributed efforts. Later in this book, we shall see and notice the need and benefits in embracing strategic initiatives and its impacts on an organisation as a whole.

Most writers and author put initiatives as an inspirational aspect of leadership, which enables leaders to view and examine situations with a critical insight and to think far ahead of others in order to communicate and give direction with any form of doubt. Segun Akinola, the founder of the 929 clothing brand, cleared the air in a seminar held in Luton few years ago, that the ability to make innovations occurs in an inspirational form, due to the desire for expansion. This may come in a form of redesigning current products or developing substitute products against current monopoly. The most common examples of such situation are automobiles, mobile phones and clothing's. The continuous flow of initiatives has brought the increasing state of competition, giving buyers more barging power and choice of taking the price and quality as the major factors. In another case, merchants would enjoy in creating a state:' either buy it or leave" (a case where the buyer has no option or say in the marketplace).

In his book "The 21 Indispensable Qualities of a Leader", Dr. John Maxwell regards a vision as something vital, that a leader should never leave the home without. However, the inability of a leader to take the right initiative at the right time and at the right place is the easiest way for a leader to be taken for granted. He stated a powerful quote from Conrad Hilton that: *"success is connected with action. Successful people keep moving. They make mistakes, but they don't quit."* Taking insights from this quote, success seems to be connected with action, i.e. success is and will be the result of taking the right action, having the relevant and accurate resources such as information, finance, location and human effort, to execute plans which are on board. It's so easy for vision to go unfulfilled and to make a mission baseless, when there is a lack of the right determination and action. Nothing will ever connect such vision with success. *"Successful people keep moving'* 'regardless of the challenges they are facing with. They always think of alternative measures in handing and overcoming situations and they keep focus on their main achievement and avoid going off course. *"They keep moving"*, doesn't mean a smooth journey but to remain on track, no matter what happens. *"They make mistakes, but they don't quit"* means that they are fearless and keep trying regardless of how many times they have failed. In most cases, their successful story is worth telling and hearing. I see people spending more time expressing their regrets of their inability to take right action during their prime years. Yet, that doesn't change the story. Initiative could still be taken at any point in time, if only the previous mistakes are overlooked and another page is opened.

Having a strategic mind and strategic mission are related because they both require the understanding of the multi tasked activities and their impact involved in making long term plans for the expansion of an organisation capacity. This is combined with developing excellence in terms of customer's and other stakeholder satisfaction on a long term basis.

Transformation as a whole is a matter of improving performance and maintaining effective leadership across an organisation. It's not all about communication or describing the big picture. It is also about understanding how to execute the right processes in achieving the strategic mission that is desired by an organisation. Another vital aspect that needs consideration in having a strategic mission is the ability to evaluate it at regular interval. This is important because it deals with the studying and monitoring of the outcome of the transformational process and other relevant factors in an extensible manner to meet the desired objectives. However, there are five major areas to be considered as this state:

A) PERFORMANCE AGAINST THE MISSION

The mission of an organization is the ultimate purpose of its existence. In order to see if an organisation is meeting its mission, leaders could measure performance in terms of time, quantity, quality of materials and the other costs involved to produce services at a regular interval. They could consider other parameters such as customer convenience, response time, or the amount of customer satisfaction in the relationship set expectations, as well. The team's performance set target in a specified period, in terms of lateness and absenteeism, which simply reflects what an organisation is attempting to fulfil more as a whole and not just what it had offered previously. In order to keep the performance at a good level, leaders should ensure that activities are kept within the parameters of the agreed strategic aims and objectives. All operational activities should be consistent with organisation's vision, mission and values. Leaders need to keep internal and external changes under review, which may require changes in the organisation's strategy or it can affect their ability to achieve their objectives within any transformational process.

B) PERFORMANCE AGAINST PROCESS.

Operational activities do require numerous processes or steps to be taken in order to provide a service or make a product. However, an organization would have to measure efficiency, effectiveness and the timeline of these processes because these elements play a key role in building or sustaining key operating systems. Processes aimed at effective performance would have to maximize staff engagement and development in a consistent manner across the organisations units. The process needs to be flexible, efficient, measurable, fair and transparent. The process also needs to review its previous performance and goals and then focus on future developments and opportunities for the purpose of its growth.

C) PERFORMANCE OF SUBSYSTEMS

These are the internal subsystems that are keys of supporting the production processes that result in specific outputs of service or products. It includes such elements as the implementation of new policies or procedures or installing a new information technology system. Such subsystems include products, services, projects and employees. Measurements include evaluating the time, effort and effectiveness of these internal systems in getting things done.

D) INDIVIDUAL PERFORMANCE MEASURES.

Individual performance measures include personal goals and objectives that are mutually agreed upon. Such as financial targets and level of customer service or satisfaction that are attached to an attractive reward. It becomes important for team members to make a personal effort in focusing on the level of quality, efficiency and quantity of service they contribute toward meeting the overall aims and objectives of an organisation. Individual measures approaches are used in meeting targets such as flexibility and supporting attitudes. Individual performance measures typically focus on the individual working to achieve results and goals while in line with the organisation's performance standard. These results and goals need to be recorded and referenced during a performance appraisal process in later date, mostly for training and development purposes because it helps to identify the needs of various individuals.

E) STAFF ALIGNMENT

If the goal is to ensure the right people are in the right place and at the right time, then organisations must measure and evaluate elements such as staff turnover, absenteeism, worker satisfaction and the cost of all recruitment efforts.

The major key of alignment is to ensure that employees understand the relevance of their contributions. It is also important to take the appropriate measures to ensure they remain engaged with the organisation as a whole. A good understanding of alignment enables a better way for setting achievable goals and remains committed to regular monitoring for the purpose of effectiveness.

The strategic mission consists of both strategic and operational objectives. It deals with turning the organisation's visions into reality and it is about achieving and understanding the strengths and weaknesses in board context. This tells how well an organization could address the needs of customers in creating new markets, and how it compares with competitor's products and services. They both make it necessary for organizations to identify, research and analyse various methods towards increasing the size, profit level and marketing segmentation. Differentiated value remains the major outcome of both objectives. In a nut-shell, strategic mission needs to be clear and easy to understand by all stakeholders anytime, anywhere. The motive behind the strategic mission should be a source of empowerment to team members, having elements of possibility, development and continuous improvement in terms of advancing the current state of an organisation.

A famous football coach granted an interview some years ago, and was asked, what he considered most during half time. He said that he saw it as an opportunity to review the team performance in relationship with the game as a whole. The outcome of the review gives an insight of where the necessary adjustment is being required. The major aim is to keep winning or to turn the situation around when the team is losing. However, for an organization to be successful in the long run, it is required to carry out a periodical strategic review to have an insight of where necessary adjustment is needed. It provides an overall view of the current performance level in the direction and purpose that the organisation desired, because it studies the previous outcomes in relationship with the current ones and checks if it's in line with the organisations desires. Due tithe changes in the external environment, such as inflation, leaders need to reassess goals at regular interval to make some realistic adjustments. Strategic review is not all about measuring and comprising performance or finding problems. It also includes finding and making improvements in ensuring lasting success. It also enables leaders to study and assess the current status of an organisation in terms of the achieved results and the impact on the organisation as a whole.

With a general point of view, organisations need to aim at maintaining its position among the best within the industry, both locally and globally. Further developing and strengthening its network within the industry is to avoid being a victim of circumstance, either as a result of changes in the law or a standard. Cooperation with other similar organisations is needed, in order to achieve maximum synergy in relation-to minimizing overhead costs or to share facilities such as joint purchases at a huge discount or issuing contracts to get services rendered as a loss. To succeed, organisations need to maintain and further develop an efficient incentive structure and well-run service functions which would be capable to support their operational priorities to give the best value for money.

"There are many tools available to help write a mission or vision statement, but I think it's often best to keep it simple -- one or two sentences -- and describe why the business exists. What is the core value or the daily purpose? Write it down and share it with everyone! Next, create an employee manual that reflects the culture." (Joanna Meiseles)

Leaders should not underestimate the importance of integrity in their strategic mission because it serves as the cornerstone in making their actions more credible in public sight. As the quote from previous page makes it clear, strategic mission talks about the organisation, and there are facts that can't be hidden. Integrity is about doing whatever promised or said and it reflects the core values an organisation stands for. Strategic mission is all about what we want to and how we can have and do it. However, understanding the law of consistency helps in reflecting the beauty of having a strategic mission because it enables one to keep on the track regardless of challenges.

PRINCIPLE 3

INFLUENCING WITHOUT AUTHORITY

"Think twice before you speak, because your words and influence will plant the seed of either success or failure in the mind of another." (Napoleon Hill)

Influencing without authority is a platform for leaders to take advantage of their communication opportunities in order to create an impact in a structured manner and in a clear form so that the results are improved continuously. This requires self-confidence and credibility. It is the ability to lead and connect with others without any form of fear or force in achieving organisational goals. It's a process of influencing others by using the emotional intelligence in order to create better working relationships, which enables the execution of projects as a team, rather than by using the power and reflecting an autocratic manner of leadership. The ability to lead others without authority is a unique approach to influence leverages concept which help leaders connect with others at a deeper level through effective planning and some other leadership techniques. However, for any leader to be able to lead without the use of authority, such would have to learn, know and understand how to establish trust, credibility with team members and other stakeholders. A leader needs to deal with everyone equally rather than being partial or operating a divide and rule system. It's about communicating in a convincing and professional manner to enable the transformational processes go easier. In a nutshell, leaders need to know the best way to attract valuable ideas and therefore build and improve their relationship with their team members. They have to exploit the current, relevant and updated models and tools for their team development. It's up to leaders to know and understand the impact they create with their actions, words or lifestyle in dealing with difficult situations and problematic personalities. Engaging and influencing would help both managers and leaders in becoming effective. There is no point in wishing to control all and not giving others a sense of belonging. Some leaders are only interested in what team members can do for them on the spot, seeking their interest and not the various methods of support members for improvement purposes. The truth about such leaders is that they are missing out on the benefit of influencing because those that are supported could later become the brain behind the strategic and operational successes, as a matter of fact.

Being simple and transparent doesn't mean that reasonable expectation could not set, but in an achievable and realistic manner. Leaders and managers need to know how to influence the behaviour of others with less formal authority and address on carrying out responsibilities as the major issue, due to the impact that needs to be created and sustained. Effective leaders are expected to know how to use informal, indirect authority to influence key stakeholders such as associates, customers, suppliers and staff. The ability to analyse situations requires influence and acknowledgment of how to build effective relationships upward, downward and laterally. That always helps in becoming a positive, powerful advocate for transformation. The ability to influence others saves both leaders and managers that are playing the hard ball game in getting things done. It also creates an avenue for inspiring stakeholders towards engagement. Another fact about influencing authority is that leaders and managers have to understand the characteristics of a successful persuader. This helps them in networking the role and importance of self-belief and courage, both within and outside the organisation. It's about learning and understanding how to build trust by looking through other people's perspectives. This is required in order to identify and understand their basic needs and the best approach in meeting those needs via the use of effective questioning techniques.

Leading without authority is about responding in a polite and reasonable manner in overcoming resistance, rather than reacting during conflicting situations. However, it is wise for leaders to adopt strategies that work for them in managing complex relationships both within and outside an organization, which enables them state their case assertively and convincingly in any situation and also maximise their personal impact.

Influencing without authority is an effective way of leading others with clear communication in terms of what an organisation expects from each stakeholder, so that things work as desired. It entails leaders to be transparent, i.e. no hidden agendas and manipulation in their relationship and dealings within and outside an organisation. This enhances more respect for leaders, both in action and words because their attitude establishes trust and makes people take them seriously.

To influence without authority, leaders need to embrace social intelligence, i.e. offering insight into interpersonal issues that interfere with work, such as building a credible network of support to help others facilitate resolution to issues they might face in the cause of their developmental process.

PRINCIPLE 4

DISCOVERING ONESELF

"Self-mastery has to start with self-honesty." (Thai Nguyen)

Asking oneself realistic and critical questions facilitates in requiring empowerment to break the inner limitation and negative belief that seems to make the situation impossible. Self-awareness is an essential aspect of leadership, because it means a lot to leaders in terms of what they stand for in any situation. It creates room for any leader to think before taking action. It's an act of improving one's abilities. It helps in identifying and improving one's skills, capability and strength in handling tough situations and facing down challenges. It's a platform in making the right decisions with acknowledgment of the blind spots and causes of error that are amounting to break down in the operating system. It requires knowledge for anyone to discover and understand what self-awareness is all about. It's about having a clear perception of one's personality which includes strengths, weaknesses, thoughts, beliefs, motivation, and emotions. It allows leaders to understand other people, what they perceive about them, their attitude and their responses to them at any point in time. Note; it enables leader to avoid being underestimated, mostly in using diplomatic approaches towards solving conflicts.

Self-awareness is a platform for building one's confidence in order to improve one's relationships, performance, and personal development, both professional and private. As a matter of fact, for anyone to lead, it is relevant to be aware of, leading and controlling oneself towards a high level of maturity, trust and credibility. Such ought to discover his weaknesses and deal with it properly. A leader needs to have strong boundaries in place i.e. a limit where they interact with stakeholders to avoid excesses. Be warm toward others, but say no when is needed. Be serious about it and remain focused in the desired direction and getting things done, which needs to be embraced with passions, as to maintain the integrity of organisational goals and missions.

Self-discovery and awareness are important characteristics that are expected of any leader because it enables for them to be seen as motivators with integrity, and to monitor one's own emotions and reactions, mostly in public outings. Leaders who take self-awareness seriously know when it's the best time to reach out for assistance, because they understand their strengths and weaknesses. That makes them successful in the long run, because it reflects a leader to be open minded and more creative. Discovering oneself is a matter of identifying the core values in one's personality because it enables leaders to adapt effective communication style in various situations and it also determines their patterns and behaviour. Leaders need to learn how to stay focused for long periods of time without getting distracted and to make connections with those around them and utilize the available opportunities at the aim of growth and development.

However, leaders need to be disciplined both at work and every other area in their life. It is a character trait that provides them the enduring focus that is necessary for strong and strategic leadership.

It is a paramount for everyone to know their capability in terms of identifying and describing the factors that are influencing their emotional responses. This enables them to develop a realistic sense of their personal abilities, qualities and strengths with the knowledge of what they can handle at any moment. It gives them a grounded sense of self-knowledge and confidence. To increase ones level of self-awareness, it's important to seek feedback on one's performance from others by asking realistic and critical questions and listening without justifying or defending one's actions.

One should learn to take unexpected feedback in good faith and seek for ways for improvements or make necessary adjustments. Self-awareness is also about gaining the additional knowledge of oneself that serves as a stepping stone towards the next level. However, it involves making the right choices and decisions in facing various situations at any point in time, and exploiting every learning opportunity to gain more insight towards development. It involves identifying the required basic skills towards effectiveness and understanding how to relate with others in different situations in the best way. According to Richard Shell, success begins with self-awareness because it enhances the ability to respond in a better manner rather than reacting and leading to unexpected conflict. Self-awareness is about having an honest assessment about ones strengths and weaknesses, i.e. dropping ones pride and ego while trying to cover up ones bad attributes as a way of pretending or visualizing oneself above others. The first step to recovery is admitting there is a problem that needs to be solved.

Self-awareness is so predominant to success and it transcends age, intelligence, education, profession, and experiences. As a matter of fact, leaders who are self-aware are far more likely to reach their goals. Others try their best to understand their personal style so they can better respond to life's challenges and opportunities in an acceptable manner. Self-awareness motivates anyone to take the best steps and actions to get where they want to be. On a serious note, there is always a huge need for transparency in self- awareness, in terms of transformation because it facilities mutual trust. It enhances the involvement of all stakeholders in form of responsibility through accurate share of information and makes leader's actions understandable in form of accountability. Transparency creates reliability and supports goal-oriented behaviour throughout an organisation.

Self-awareness requires one to be independent minded and maintain a high level of neutrality. A self-aware person avoids being biased or easily influenced by any situation, emotions of others and previous experiences. Self-awareness is about making introspections to benefit from personal insight. It helps people discover more about their strengths, personality traits, and intelligence, reflecting on their ability to cope under pressure and in any situation. This facilitates personal development, maturity, growth and improvement, all of which become relevant and applicable when handling situations and facing challenges, especially when managing teams or leading organisations.

Another vital point about self-awareness is that it helps in understanding one's direction better and in making one's vision a reality. In my view, self-awareness is not only about having a strategic mind-set and mission, but also about being authentic because it enables others to see one as genuine and not a copycat. It also enables one to ask oneself the critical questions and give the required answer to various situations facing one's career and private life. Experiences from self-awareness can be used in developing, equipping, and coaching others. However, for the principle of self-awareness to have a real impact, it needs to abide by the Law of Focus according to the 7 laws of productivity. It's about getting things done one thing at a time and following one course until it becomes successful. To round it on self-awareness, it facilitates the ability to redirect negative thoughts and emphasize positive ones because the power of self-discovery enables anyone to think and strive towards turning things around for the better and avoid considering defeat or abide in vacuums created by rivals which only end up producing a can of worms. Self-awareness enables anyone to live a courageous life and above limitation.

PRINCIPLE 5

IDENTIFYING AND EMBRACING STRATEGIC INITIATIVES

"A satisfied customer is the best business strategy of all."
(Michael LeBoeu)

The only thing that enables organisations to succeed in a time of disruptive changes is the provision of exceptional leadership, vision, and organisational development expertise, which requires the ability of leaders to identify and embrace strategic initiatives. Strategic initiatives need to be realistic in order to stand the test of time, mostly in the terms of revolutionary changes, to make new approaches worthwhile. In a nut-shell, strategic initiative could be referred to as any project or situation that combines strategic problem, solving parameters and focused leadership development. All of that is focused on achieving sustainable success, on both solutions and skills that are built over a long period of time.

Initiatives are special forms of actions that organisation

undertake to implement its strategy. This is based on relevant and accurate intelligence gotten about competitor's activities and available opportunities that could be exploited for strategic benefits. It also concerns the best way to face down challenges that might surface during the strategy development process. It's about creating value and uniqueness which is always a result of gaining and developing the insight of inventing something new or different from something that already exists. Leaders need to take initiatives in order to make the key decisions about enhancing accomplishments of the organization. Initiatives are the major efforts that are required to take strategic progress toward its goals that needs to be clarified during the implementation process.

In 1903, Henry Ford, the founder of the Ford Motor Company, had the initiative of producing automobiles that middle class Americans could afford. Until then, automobiles were regarded as hand-tooled and customized toy for the rich people and leading car firms decided to keep that way. So Henry Ford never found it easy or funny when he had to face a lot of legal battles by then leading car manufactures who tried to put him out of business. But he had gone a long way in the battle with the other manufacturers simply because they wanted the cars to be just for the rich, and he did not. His initiative later made a huge impact to the judge, so they made it clear that the simple fact that Henry Ford had an initiative that is different from other manufactures does not apply any laws to ban his product in any form. This shows that embracing an initiative distinguishes an organisation in the marketplace and creates more opportunity for its growth.

The process of embracing strategic initiatives needs to be closely related to having clarity of the overall plan and goal that describes the purpose and priorities in a clear concise manner. The issue of who and when in terms of getting things done, needs to be clarified to avoid conflict and each role and responsibility needs to be in line with the overall strategic objective. Although strategic initiative enhances clarity that is required to edge out competitors in the marketplace, it still needs to be made in terms of setting and communicating organisational directions.

The burning desire of strategic initiatives must adapt, transform in order to achieve previously unattainable performance and success in the face of increasing pressure and competition. Meanwhile, leaders need to operate with a democratic leadership style and communicate with others to discover raw statements in the form of personal option. They need to have an in-depth view of regular occurring issues, which gives a possible and lasting solution to the situations that are a challenge for the organisation. However, identifying strategic initiatives does not grant success, but the ability to communicate and execute it, which needs to be embraced by stakeholders. That is what makes the initiative transform an organisation. In clear terms, when a good vision lacks the required support, it fails. This issue is similar to the story about the popular trader that was selling a product for the most reasonable price, but the donkey he relied on to convey those products to customers felt sick on the business day. Since there was no substitute, he lost it all.

A good initiative needs to possess the power of strategy and innovation in order to be transformative. It needs to have a developmental and personalized approach because initiatives work differently in various organizations and at different time or situations, i.e. an initiative might be transformative in firm A and destructive in firm B.

However, strategic initiative needs to enhance strategic intent, i.e. the readily grasped declaration of the course that the management of a particular organisation wishes to execute in taking it for a certain time frame. It has to be in the interest of all stakeholders and must be able to transform an organisation from its current state to a desired one.

The best side of every strategic initiative is the ability to be evaluated and to be implemented in a consistent manner.

The processes of evaluation enable leaders to compare and contrast situations objectively and make effective decisions based on the entire need for adaptation and implementation. However, strategic initiatives need to be evaluated in three dimensions, i.e. strategic alignment, economic value, and risk assessment.

Strategic alignment ensures that the strategy is the best fit in the relationship to the situation that is to be applied to get the best results in terms of service delivery. In a nut - shell, the major components to watch for in strategic alignment are its ability to serve a better competitive edge and creating a better avenue for organizational development.

Competitive edge determines the extents from which the initiative could increase an organization's position in the market from. It is also about the power of an organization's brand to create the required awareness so more clients or customers are attracted. However, the initiative needs to process the capability to give the best value in terms of service to customers and the ability to increase an organization's market share, as well.

Organisational Development is about the extent strategic initiative which can reinforce the desired culture, enhance stakeholder relations, increase relevant knowledge and enable an organization to function more effectively in order to accomplish more successful organizational changes and performances.

Economic value is a monetary value analysis that determines whether an initiative has the financial capability to get the best of an investment and provide quantifiable measurements to evaluate against expected cost. Information about the costs needs to be relatively straightforward. They also need to create room for adjustments on items such as maintenance, renewal, and internal resource costs, which are usually left out during budgeting. Economic value deals with the Payback Period, or Breakeven Period, which reflects the timeframe it takes for an initiative to yield a positive cumulative cash flow.

Return on Investment (ROI) is an economic value which provides the percentage return that an investment would generate within a timeframe.

Net Present Value (NPV) gives the present value of a future stream of cash flows by discounting the future cash flows against the cost of capital or any other preferred rate.

It is a measure of the net benefit of an initiative in today's money. NPV is useful because it provides the magnitude of the value, but not the magnitude of an investment. Internal Rate of Return (IRR) takes the cash flow schedule of the initiative without discounting the cash flow into account. It provides a break-even rate of return where the NPV is zero. In other words, if the cost of capital equals the IRR there is no economic value from the investment. An IRR rate level is often used as a hurdle rate for initiatives.

Risk Assessment could be measured and based on the probability of an unexpected occurrence and possible mitigation. The measurement of risks can be used as a stand-alone quantitative measure or be translated into a discounted value that is used in the economic value analysis. Risk could occur in different forms and anytime, in terms of customer perspective and external events that may occur unexpectedly and decrease the attractiveness of the organization's value for current and potential customers. Process perspective might be affected negatively and an organization might be unable to create value as promised to consumers and other stakeholders. The role of risk management and assessment should never be underestimated due to its ability to identify possible risks and reduce it, what makes it naturally strategic because it enhances planning ahead.

Assessing and managing risks are the best weapon anyone could have against project catastrophes. Evaluating ones plan for potential problems and developing strategies to address them, increases ones chances of being successful.

Leaders need to ensure that high priority risks are aggressively managed and that all risks are cost-effectively managed throughout a transformational process.

To hit home, embracing strategic initiatives need to serve as an embodiment of learning and growth because it enables leaders to indicate if customer's needs are met, i.e. level of satisfaction and utility derived from consuming their product. The business processes create room for improvement towards achieving organizational goals with available resources and shows how far financial goals are being achieved for the purpose of strategic planning. This is also important for keeping and maintaining the organization in better state, regardless of external influences. For any strategic initiatives succeed it is required that the right information is allocated in the right portion and at the right time in order to reflect the value and impact within an organization.

There is no need to use initiatives until either leaders or managers are faced with specific and critical organizational challenge such as implementing a new strategy, designing and launching a new product, integrating an acquisition, resolving a conflict between functions, or even helping a new leader to build his/her team. The role and impact of such initiatives would hardly be recognized.

Initiatives can also be used as the vehicle for developing and embracing new technologies in order to get things done faster and to select high potential talents. Embracing the right initiatives helps the organization to set up the right brand in promoting its services and its mission. It also increases the awareness and understanding of the general public in giving them the real value for their money. Another importance of embracing and supporting initiatives is that it enhances innovation and improvement practices by evaluating current trends and encouraging more efficient and effective approaches within the industry.

Leaders need to understand that for initiative to be seen as genuine; it needs to focus on solving the actual problem and should possess the ability and durability to be integrated with relevant operating plans. The process needs to be understood by all stakeholders and it needs to be smart and simple. All relevant information needs to be at hand and potential result needs to be achievable. It's advisable for leaders to embrace initiatives that encourage a culture of change because that fosters talents and increases capabilities of an organization. Transformation is likely to be achieved only when stakeholders have the leader's genuine support for execution activities. Taking initiative requires one starting small and learns fast where possible, the initiative needs to be result oriented by creating room for growth and improvement.

What would be the result of a particular initiative and how would success be measured are major considerations that leaders need to deliberate on before execution. Who is responsible and involved in getting things done and what steps are required to achieve the desirable outcome. Taking Initiative enables leaders to take courage and build self-confidence, especially when others disagree due to fear of the unknown and lack of courage.

Strategically leading, in terms of taking initiatives enables leaders to understand the possible overcome of various key challenges that come at various points and times of the transformational process. The desire for transformation in meeting and facing down challenges makes leaders build the required framework, which could enable successful steering of their strategic initiatives to produce the desired and expected result. Strategic initiatives enable leaders to gain insight into the drivers of successful execution by linking it to the overall strategy. Leaders need to create a compelling vision for their initiative, access and manage crucial stakeholder relationships and build the required momentum for transformation to be realistic. Identifying and embracing strategic initiatives creates a stronger platform for innovation that leads to new dimensions of performance. Innovation involves taking intelligent risks at all operations, systems, and processes to get the values of all organizing efforts because the end would always justify the means. Similar to jigsaw puzzle, innovation needs to be integrated into organizational operations in order to facilitate improvement in overall performance and systems that needs to be done in the organisation.

Leaders who believe in embracing strategic initiatives are well known for inspiring others, because their works speaks for them ,whether they are still alive or not. The story of Volkswagen Beetle was a result of Ferdinand Porsche that was inspired by Henry Ford, i.e. producing a vehicle that could be affordable to an average German, which brought up the invention of Ford cars. The ability of solving a particular is the beauty of embracing an initiative.

It's very important for an initiative to process elements of effective execution on a strategic base which makes it meaningful, acceptable and actionable. For a strategic initiative to be executable, two things must be true. First, the strategy must be meaningful to the people who will execute it. The organization's mission must be embedded in the initiative. The objectives must be clear. The strategy should provide a rallying cry for every stakeholder within the organization. Second, the strategy must be actionable and reasonable.

At the end, every organization will have its own strategy to execute, either to be offensive or defensive but what distinguishes initiatives from each other is the value that it creates. As a matter of fact, leaders need to bear in mind the huge need to always execute the value, because that's the only indicator of achievements that derive from an initiative. That could help in setting up basics for the future execution processes and also in increasing organizations' commitment and confidence of stakeholders.

In order to execute a particular strategy effectively, leaders must successfully plan and understand their strategic initiatives, knowing both positive and negative impacts that could be created, mostly when a faulty situation occurs unexpectedly. The beauty of every initiative lies in the ability of it to be executed and made materialistic, reflecting a clear connection between strategic choices and sustainable competitive advantage over rivals.   It also must be understandable and motivated to all stakeholders across an organization for a better future. To cut the long story short, embracing an initiative is not thought worthwhile as the ability of leader's to stick through tougher times is. Such leaders are provided with knowledge of what they want and doing so in regards of transformation an organization.

PRINCIPLE 6

BUILDING AND PROTECTING ORGANIZATION BRAND

"A brand for a company is like a reputation for a person. You earn reputation by trying to do hard things well."(Jeff Bezos)

In a situation where products in the market seem to be similar in size and colour, being guided by a legal standard, organizations need to work hard to establish a unique identity that resonates with consumers and adds value to the company's portfolio of goods and services. The only way to differentiate a product once it arrives, the marketplace is its brand, which reflects the quality and value which consumers derive as a result of its uniqueness. However, it needs to be substantial, recognized and well respected and protected. A brand can be used as a weapon to minimize confusion among similar products in the sight of consumers due to its established and unique identity. It does help organization to reinforce the difference from competitors and can help to encourage and also increase customer loyalty. However, the brand of an organization is an example of intellectual property, which needs to be one of the most valuable assets an organization needs to protect, due to its huge impact on it. Organisational stakeholders need to Identify and understand the quality values and customer experiences associated with an organizational brand, which makes it more credible and not just a slogan or a logo.

Knowing the role and importance of a brand, leaders need to conduct some research to ensure that no organization is already using the proposed brand before investing and settling on it. Another fact on branding is the ability to protect it by registering to avoid infringement where no leader should spare any expense or energy from. Protection includes setting clear standards on how the brand should be used both internally and externally and communicated from within, as well as by other partners or any other third party. Tim Jones, a marketing expert, said that there is a need for leaders to set a reasonable standard for the use of organizational brands by a third party which could be in the form of controlling and monitoring alongside specific terms and conditions to avoid negative publication from the media.

However, the strongest form of protection for a brand is a registered trade mark which distinguishes products or services of a particular organization from others regardless of time and location. It's important for leaders to communicate through the organizational brand in terms of what it stands for, i.e. quality of products and value given back to customers in terms of money, and how it arrived, i.e. the ability to satisfy customer's needs. However, brands need to be promoted alongside with reasonable time and financial reasons. New brands are introduced in the market and this should be handled by a marketing campaign that includes press releases, PR and advertising, special offers and promotions to customers. It could be promoted by making it visible on stationery materials, website and marketing materials. Leaders should never underestimate or neglect customer perceptions about an organization's product, as it is very vital in protecting their real image and reputation, which remains as assets as far the organization exist. There is a huge need to be consistent in spreading the good news and success attached to the organization's brand. That way their uniqueness in the marketplace are created and this helps in maintaining a better position. A brand reflects the trust in a particular product or service and that is also a tool to convince other potential customers and clients. It is always advisable for organisation to watch out from misusing or operating their brand illegally. Once a brand is blacklisted by the media, it creates a negative image and huge doubt between both existing and potential clients and to correct the affected situation costs both time and money. Branding should always be a corporate strategic issue and not a short-term tactical activity. An organization that wants to satisfy the needs of consumers and edge out competitors, need to build a brand with a reasonable image that provides an attractive opportunity for business expansion and profit maximization with a serious minded slogan. This could help an organization to defy the test of time and make it limitless to their operations and life expectancy. Brands could last longer than its investor. And in most cases, they do because they are a legacy, similar to some well-known and established brands, such as Marlboro, Nescafe, Hewlett-Packard, Nestle and Siemens, which are immemorial and still have a lion share in the marketplace.

Another vital aspect when building and protecting a brand is the ability of leaders to attract customer loyalty. This enables organizations to achieve a greater consistency of demand through customer retention by sticking to their promise in terms of value, derived for preferring their product. Leaders need to continuously seek and develop various strategies in the retention of its customer loyalty. A particular car park, service and a former market leader in the United Kingdom was once forced to change its brand, due to a huge number of motorists and local residents 'complains. This later became the major news headline on both digital and printed media, which made local councils and partnering organizations to disassociate themselves due the negative reports. An investigation later revealed that the directors had deliberately imposed a huge number of penalty charge notices per quarter to be issued on various contract managers with the aim of keeping its existing clients and generate more. This was the major reason for its traffic warrens carry on issuing a huge number of ghosts and controversial charge notices to drivers due to the compulsory individual targets that were set to avoid termination of appointment. On the long run, the government had to intervene in the alarming situation. The worst occurred when some of its former employee's, both managers and officers later came on air to expose some of their wrong and unlawful practices. In light of many unanswered questions, the organisation's reputation was damaged, which resulted in a loss of many of their clients. The sad news was that their rivals won most of their terminated contracts and wisely secured long term deals, which had left the former market leaders slugging, regardless of its new name and brand.

In a nut–shell, a well-protected brand would always have a positive impact on the organisation, mostly in the aspect of negotiations about the cost, quality and quantity, because making better deals would be easier. Suppliers and customers would like to associate themselves with a well-respected organisation to boost their chances of generating more clients and businesses. There lies a treasure that needs to be kept and maintained.

Another major fact about a brand is that it reflects not just the product (which is to be sold to the customer), but also the experience required to maintain the top position within the industry. McDonald's is a very good example because the company believes in not just selling fast food but selling quality food fast with the aim of delivering maximum satisfaction. This is one of the main reasons why organisational leaders need to be very conscious of their brand strategy because it helps in them take huge leaps compared to their rivals. A typical example of this was the difference of 27 billion dollars McDonald's was able edge over its rival Burger King, in 2012. According to my strategic management lecturer, McDonald's was able to form the brand with the consultation of 47 children psychologists from different parts of the world. The brand has established an attractive image not just for children but also for investors who pay a large amount of money to acquire its franchise due to the value brand created over the years in public sight. To get the best value of a specific brand on a continuous base, leaders need to analyse how their organisational brand is positioned within the market and crystallise targeted consumers because, technically, a brand is an organisation in itself. Leaders need to provide the accurate and realistic vision, mission, goals and strategies to match such brand with other leaders in the market. Another aspect of positioning a particular brand for strategic benefits is the ability of leaders and managers to monitor market trends as well as research consumer markets and competitors' activities to identify opportunities and key issues which enhances the best strategic decision to edge out rivals. For an organisation to benefit from a consistent strategy and clear mission, it's wise to ensure that marketing and advertising activities are well overseen. However, it's up to leaders to monitor product distribution and consumer reactions to get rid of bottlenecks and brainstorm innovative competitive and growth strategies to keep an organisation at the peak within the marketplace. Establishing internal performance specifications, such as cost and price parameters, market applications and sales estimates are other useful function, which enable organisations to build and protect their brands from their rivals. However, this requires taking action in the marketplace, which is never a funfair but warfare.

PRINCIPLE 7

EMBRACING INSPIRATIONAL LEADERSHIP

"If your actions inspire others to dream more, learn more, do more and become more, you are a leader."
(John Quincy Adams)

It is paramount for leaders to consider and understand the social and political environment where they operate and intend to stay for a while. This will enable them to establish the right type of organisational changes that is required of them in transforming situations to reality. Understanding the environment and other determinable parameters such as logistics, availability of labour and resources would enable leaders to identify the issues at certain period of time and choose their preferred strategy or method of operating in that environment. In most cases leaders need to be effective and strategic at decision making and considering if they should operate in a specific environment on a short or long term bases. Transforming an organisation inspirational leadership is highly recommended because it's about applying the right insight and making others understand the purpose and benefit of transformational exercise, at a particular time and for the right reason. Inspirational leadership is about considering the appropriateness of leader's responses to the leadership required in handing unexpected situation and not waving from reality or failing to give real answers at critical questions. It enables leaders to develop an approach for creating a true engagement in sharing their commitment by reflecting and applying their knowledge and experience in supporting others towards improvement and transformation. It creates the platform for embracing and developing new mentalities towards innovation in terms of its acceptance and support.

Inspirational Leadership is about energizing and creating a sense of direction and purpose for organisational stakeholders along with the excitement and momentum for change. I see inspirational leadership as the best approach towards transformation. It involves energizing individuals to strive towards a compelling vision for the future and embracing and embodying organization values in all aspects of their contributing efforts. It offers clarity around goals and objectives and ensures that those who lead execute strategies with an effective team spirit towards a common goal. It also includes the provision of the required resources and motivational support for team members to experience growth and empowerment through delegation in their respective fields. This makes possible for them to reach their full potential, create more space of improvement and take responsibility for their own success, which makes it easier to hold them accountable.

Inspirational Leadership as a whole promotes respect, dignity and integrity within the organisation. It recognizes both individuals and team achievements in terms of knowledge and capabilities that are shared in achieving a specific level of excellence. Inspirational Leadership is also about using leadership to facilitate fairness and trust in a way that team members are feeling appreciated and valued for their unique contribution.

It's about leaders being opened to other's ideas or seeing others as influential figures, regarding them as real stakeholders and believing that they have something valuable to say or offer, regardless of the position(s) they hold.

Another benefit of inspirational leadership is its ability to create a safe environment for learning, giving and receiving feedback, because it becomes easier to suggest possible necessary changes, mostly when current solutions and approaches are no longer applicable.

Coaching remains an important aspect of Inspirational Leadership because it enhances the development of others by providing constructive feedback and showing sensitivity to diversity in terms of individual needs. It enables leaders, managers and coaches share their own experience and knowledge in attaining best practice with others for the purpose of motivating and assisting in their on-going development process. Coaching is another and major platform in promoting the understanding of transformation along with its positive impact to bring stakeholders to an accord and to reduce the rate of resistance or negative reaction of change that occurred in the organisation.

It becomes easier to foster group cohesion, shared purpose and engagement once an organisation embraces inspirational leadership. It serves as a stimulant that accelerates positive energy into the activities of an organisation as a whole. It takes for a leader to be inspirational in order to communicate transformation and its process with a collective purpose and to give a clear line of insight to an organisation's value proposition or future agenda. Inspirational leaders always consider that it is important to involve others in planning and implementation in order to enable them gain a 'buy-in' platform, which makes it easier to deal with any form of resistance to change. They also need to make it clear to stakeholders why the transformation is required at a particular time, its benefits, what is at stake, the possible outcomes and impact it has on them and the organization as a whole.

Inspirational Leadership help organisations to build enthusiasm for change because it generates excitement, enthusiasm and commitment of stakeholders by translating the organization's vision, mission and values in terms that are relevant to high performance leadership. It also helps in translating organisational strategies into specific and practical goals and processes within a reasonable time frame due to the ability of a leader to communicate the big picture.

Inspirational Leadership combines clarity of purpose with personal conviction, optimism and a sense of determination for leaders to be at their very best and to be seen as role models. It helps an organisation to demonstrate a genuine passion and value for research and development, which is the major cornerstone of innovation and transformation. It also inspires the commitment within an organisation by continuously providing insight and real leadership for others to execute the best strategies that could transform an organization from its current state to its future desired state or success level.

However, leaders are also required to take reasonable actions to ensure that others understand and endorse the required organisational strategies that could create value and perfect engagement with both internal and external stakeholders. This helps in attaining better relationship with its alliance that assists organizational executions in an authentic and effective approach.

Inspirational Leadership is about genuine listening and addressing to any concerns about the future of an organisation, which enables leaders to promote a climate of continuous transformation, to keep it agile and "the best in class." It also enables leaders to reinforce the vision of change and ensures that the organizational processes and practices are accordingly aligned. It's about leading and inspiring others to create something truly innovative and distinguishing among others competitors.

Without any form of doubt Inspirational Leadership embraces transparency, which enables that all stakeholders have access in making decisions. It's not about releasing all of the confidential information or withholding it unnecessarily. It is about leaders being honest, direct and clear about their motives and also sharing relevant information with the rightful stakeholders, at the right time.

Inspirational leaders are well known for possibly making attempts in connecting with others to avoid being out of touch. This is a platform for establishing the tee in order to gain team members' commitment, which is very important. Inspirational leaders are the people who literally inspire those around them in achieving a great goal. They are much more than great motivators and charismatic icons. They are the ones who believe in creating impact consistently towards greatness and making transformation a reality. Inspirational leadership enables leaders to carry members along with the insight, hope and courage, regardless of what the situation might be faced with, and not making them feel the fear of the unknown.

Embracing inspirational leadership is about accountability, i.e. leaders considering themselves responsible for the achievements and success within an organisation asa whole and also responsible for their inability to deliver expectations. It is about fostering an environment of mutual respect and building a trust among stakeholders, respecting and valuing each other's ideas and not dominating issues in their interest. On a serious note, leaders need to inspire others towards making contributions and suggestions based on their experience, which are also platforms towards transformation.

WHY TRANSFORMATION EFFORTS FAIL

Having conducted my research from different sources, I realize that no matter how intelligent leaders and their team may be, *mistake has no master*. The same parameters that determine the success in situation A can be the major cause of failure in situation B. It is up to the organizations to ensure transformation success by avoiding pitfalls. Having the right initiative is one thing, while having the right sponsorship is another, as it could determine the extent of the transformational process. It is about embracing the objectives that are easier to achieve. For any vision to embark on a mission, it always requires time and money, which is the major reason why leaders should always ensure an accurate budget in executing a project and a reasonable time limit in order to avoid a possible negative effect on a transformational process.

Poor communication is another reason why transformation fails, because once stakeholders are unable to understand the big picture, leaders would have to struggle for their support, which enhances a huge tendency of failure in the long run. Without team members that are in a better medical, physiological and emotional state, huge mistakes and damages would occur, which increases the level of stress, illness, sleepless nights, anger, loss of self-confidence, and general disillusionment within an organisation. It also affects the quality of execution and frustrates transformation as a whole.

Studying both local and international economic trends, effective leaders should be able to predict likely changes in external drives, such as market price index, inflation and other external factors. According to Dr. John Kotter's article *'Leading Change',* he explained further why transformation efforts do fail on a long run. I would like to explain five of them:

1. Distrust of Leadership: transformational leadership would always have to entail trust, in order to inspire and carry others along, because no leader earns the commitment of his team if he is misleading them, i.e. continually breaking their promises.

2. Failure to Engage Stakeholders: it's not all about engaging any stakeholder but the right stakeholders at various points of an organisational process. However, various stakeholders got various interests, which is the major reason why leaders must learn effective negotiation skills and to carefully analyse stakeholders' requirements and expectations to avoid conflicts.

3. Inadequate Resource Allocation: Before communicating a vision, leaders need to conduct a thorough assessment of resources, i.e. time, people, funds, equipment and processes involved in making an initiative come to life.

4. Lack of Learning: Institutional changes are important, and this should include a review of lessons that are learned and collected throughout the initiative, in order to enhance the growth and development. Without learning, it becomes hard to train and coach others within an organization.

5. Miscommunication: This is explained in a previous stage of this book, yet there is a huge need for improvement.

To avoid failure in the transformational process, leaders and managers need to learn how to effectively manage and control themselves through organizational changes, in order to maximize personal leadership impact. Another way is to acquire the right skills to lead their team through change and ensuring continuous engagement and productivity by giving the necessary support. They must identify and navigate common pitfalls associated with the transformational process and get rid of them. In order to improve their organisation, leaders need to know the best way to ensure the cohesiveness of their team by utilizing influence instead of authority.

TAKE THIS HOME

My candid advice to any leader or anyone aiming at transforming an organisation or any situation for the better, should avoid making strategic decisions while under intense pressure or in the midst of controversy due to unexpected implications. However, it's paramount for trends to be well studied in relationship to the future of an organisation because its more expensive than exiting from a strategy already in motion other than carrying on implementing the same strategy. And in the midst of controversy, native intelligence i.e. knowledge gained through personal experience could be applied in handing complex situations towards achieving the expected results.

Transformational leaders need to know and understand, regardless of the situation might be, transformation requires sacrifice i.e. giving up today's pleasure for tomorrow's comfort. The transformation might need changing the organization's direction, increasing its quality level, creating a new image or building a new reputation. Achieving transformation is never and would never be easy. Dr. Moses Solaru, my long-time mentor once told me:' *Being defeated is often temporary, giving up makes it permanent. Never give up on what you are pursuing. Many of people's life's failures is the situation where they didn't realize how close they were to their success when they gave up; keep on trying and God will crown your efforts with a resounding success."* This quote inspires me a lot and it enables me to have the mind-set of thriving and not just surviving.

A particular country in Asia, discovered the need for transformation many years ago, because it was clear that the country would remain in their unsatisfactory state if a change is not made. As a matter of fact, the government began to send their citizens abroad to educate themselves and gain a proper insight of how things are processed and worked out positively, which is a better way of equipping their next generation for future challenges. A few years after, their citizens returned and were appointed as advisers to the government at various levels. They helped the government with new ideas in transforming the state's economy, introducing e-governance, and improving the welfare of their citizens by adopting new and effective systems of the western world. They learned how to control and manage administration from government resources and projects. This also helped the government to develop and negotiate effective relationship with other countries. Transformation wouldn't have been a reality, if the government had not given the required sacrifice. The same country is now a mega city with a stable economy, a land of great opportunity, and its global investment and international trade are on the rise. The government challenged its citizens to come with a comprehensive plan to modernize the economy and improve public services and governance as a whole.

Leaders need to understand the framework of transformational leadership and how to enact behaviours within that framework that suit their own personal leadership style and abilities. They also need to know how they are perceived as leaders with their direct assessment and reports, which will help them identify grey areas for their personal leadership development and improvement. They need to understand the condition for effective goal setting, along with the implementation plan for achieving those goals.

Transformational leadership as a whole encourages authentic solutions for organizational problems in practical terms. It encourages effective performance from team members and makes them more loyal in their stewardship. Transformational leadership helps an organisation to create a supportive environment where responsibility and credit for effective performance are both shared rather than seeking personal interests and end up in a one horse race. It does Influences high level performance within an organisation and impact beyond expectations.

Another important aspect of transformational leadership is its strategy and its approach towards implementation. Leaders need to understand every aspect of their strategic initiative as well as what is the best way to meet future challenges, which should stand the test of time mostly during the formulating stage. Leaders should always seize the opportunity to motivate and inspire team members, especially when an organisation is facing a challenge or change in direction. This provides a sense of purpose which could unite team members in achieving a common set of goals. However, transformational strategies sometimes do not work out or suffer a major drawback because some leaders are used to depending on the results of previous capability or efforts in terms of how issues were handled and fixed, neglecting the variance in times and situations. This is the major reason why leaders need to discover and develop the required intellectuals to make operational strategies work successfully on a continuous basis to aid business unit and corporate strategies to keep an organisation on the defensive side.

Service through teamwork is the major pillar of transformational leadership, where leaders need to collaborate effectively with team members in order to give shareholders and other stakeholders their best performance, in terms of making their investments pay off. Transformational leaders need to understand the needs of their clients and customers as well as the need to surpass stakeholder's expectations regardless of what their role is. Transformational leaders need to aim at embracing excellence in terms of achievement and should create an environment that could enable them to attract and keep the best people who share organizational values. Transformational leaders need to embrace integrity, which enables them to act fairly, ethically and opened to every stakeholder and show the required courage to get the right thing. To hit home, transformational leadership emphasis on vision, team member's empowerment and challenging the traditional model of getting things done.

To draw the cotton at this stage, as Albert Einstein, the German-born theoretical physicist once said:' *The value of a man resides in what he gives and not in what he is capable of receiving.* " Following that, I strongly believe the worth of a man is never reflected by his age but rather in his ability to stand up to challenges in the time of pressure and by transforming the situation that is in the interest of all. Transformation would always require a reasonable time so that the effective decisions are made for its processes in order to materialize and produce the desired result. However, it falls down on leaders to plan and make use of time effectively because once it's gone, it never returns. Stakeholder's expectation is not opened for failure and only a consistent successful record makes a leader's story worth telling and hearing.

Regardless of the status or expertise level of those that are handling transformational processes, they need to be extremely careful because the result of competition should never be taken for granted, i.e. push and pull, the higher the leader aims for, the lower rivals would like to place such leader. In addition, there are some habits that make leaders more transferable, both within and outside an organisation. The ability to transform any organisation reflects effectiveness and efficiency to handle processes, programs and relevant situations competently with available resources. It also goes along with the ability to deliver expectations in light of both internal and external pressures, which requires leaders to cultivate specific habits like prioritizing time effective i.e. identify and use the available time for more important and relevant events. They can also learn from other successful leaders in terms of their skills and strategies how to give the best performance at all times by adapting. Leaders should embrace networking with other professionals in their field so that they could be updated and avoid missing opportunities. Maintaining a good working-life balance is another major aspect to be considered because it helps in keeping the body and soul fit to carry out activities in a perfect way. Also, it is important to balance the demands by remaining physically, mentally, spiritually fit in order to get things done as expected. The desire to get things done helps in building confidence and it needs to available or the invested efforts could be wasted in the long run. Transformational leaders should never think, aim or settle for less, i.e. avoiding fear or intimidation in any situation and always have the courage to remain committed towards higher achievement, i.e. strive for something bigger than oneself. Transformational leaders are well known to be peacekeepers and shooters. A very good example is the former president of Nigeria and a member of the well-known organizations "Black nation", Goodluck Ebele Azikiwe Jonathan. He conceded defeat for the sake of peace by claiming that.' Nobody's ambition is worth the blood of any Nigerian." This made him an icon in Nigerian history On a final note, the most important part of transformational leadership is helping the organisation to increase its return on investment and contributing positively to the life of an organsational's human factor. This means utilizing every financial resources effectively, improving individual and team performance in the long run and reducing the level of resistance and sabotage. It is also vital to enhance higher collaboration with other leaders and to create synergies in the organization and a strong and localized culture for growth and effective performance. As I usually say, the time to make an important change happen, create positive impact and improve unpleasant situations within an organisation and in one's private life would never occur by magic or chance, it needs to created, and else the story remains the same. There is a huge comfortability in carrying on doing the same thing which ends up making one stagnant. However, the only solution to this is standing out from the crowd with a reformed mind-set, embrace an initiative and set a new direction for oneself considering it as a strategic mission which enables one to create a positive and meaningful impact in one's life and in others as well.

www.ingramcontent.com/pod-product-compliance
Lightning Source LLC
Chambersburg PA
CBHW072054290426

44110CB00014B/1673